$\mathscr{E}$DIBLE $\mathscr{G}$IFTS

IRRESISTIBLE TREATS TO GIVE FROM THE PANTRY

LORENZ BOOKS
LONDON • NEW YORK • SYDNEY • BATH

This edition published in the UK in 1997 by Lorenz Books

Lorenz Books is an imprint of
Anness Publishing Limited
Hermes House
88-89 Blackfriars Road
London SE1 8HA

© 1997 Anness Publishing Limited

ISBN 1 85967 546 8

A CIP catalogue record for this book is available from the British Library

Publisher: Joanna Lorenz
Project Editor: Fiona Eaton
Designer: Lilian Lindblom
Jacket Designer: Harriet Athay
Jacket Photographer: Michelle Garrett
Illustrations: Anna Koska

Printed and bound in China

1 3 5 7 9 10 8 6 4 2

CONTENTS

INTRODUCTION

Much of the pleasure of cooking lies in sharing the delicious results with your family and friends. As well as putting sensational meals on the table for them, you can pamper your family and delight your friends with gifts from your kitchen that both look and taste sumptuous.

Hand-made chocolates and sweets (candies) give you an opportunity to bestow real luxury in an affordable way. It is also a great pleasure to select ingredients of the highest quality which are lovely to work with and produce finished gifts that you know will be absolutely delicious – and as good as anything money can buy.

Most satisfying of all are the treats made from produce that you have grown yourself, or perhaps collected from the hedgerows. When you are making fruit preserves with summer gluts from your garden, make enough to give some as presents. Pot your jams and jellies in pretty jars that will make them look their best,

and top them with decorative fabric or paper covers. A jewel-like jar of apple jelly or some vibrant strawberry jam will make a lovely small gift, or could be included in a basket of other home-made goodies.

For the enthusiastic cook, you could put together gourmet delights that will be useful in the kitchen and perhaps inspire some new recipes. Herb-flavoured oils or fruit vinegars are always a delight to receive. If you give herb or spice mixes, add a hand-written label with suggestions for their use, or you could include a favourite recipe of your own.

Traditional recipes are associated with every seasonal celebration of the year, from Easter eggs to the symbolic harvest loaf. There is no nicer way to mark these annual festivities than with thoughtful gifts lovingly prepared in your own kitchen.

TOMATO CHUTNEY

*If you grow your own tomatoes, it is a pleasure to share them with
your family and friends. This spicy chutney is delicious with a selection of
cheeses and biscuits, or with cold meats.*

MAKES 1.75 KG (4 LB)

*900 g (2 lb) tomatoes, skinned
225 g (8 oz/1⅓ cups) raisins
225 g (8 oz) onions, chopped
225 g (8 oz/1⅛ cups) caster
(superfine) sugar
600 ml (1 pint/2½ cups) malt
vinegar*

1 Chop the tomatoes roughly.
Put them into a preserving pan.

2 Add the raisins, chopped onions
and caster (superfine) sugar to
the pan.

TIP
Sterilize the jars by heating them
in the oven at 150°C/300°F/Gas 2
for 15 minutes.

3 Pour over the vinegar. Bring to
the boil and leave to simmer
for 2 hours, uncovered. Spoon into
warmed, sterilized jars and seal
immediately. Store in a cool,
dark place.

KASHMIR CHUTNEY

Almost every family has a few recipes for pickles and preserves that have been passed down from generation to generation. This one, with its Anglo-Indian provenance, is a wonderful accompaniment to grilled sausages.

MAKES 2.75 KG (6 LB)

1 kg (2¼ lb) green apples
15 g (½ oz) garlic cloves
1 litre (1¾ pints/4 cups) malt vinegar
450 g (1 lb) dates
115 g (4 oz) preserved ginger
450 g (1 lb/2 ½ cups) seeded raisins
450 g (1 lb/2 cups) brown sugar
2.5 ml (½ tsp) cayenne pepper
25 g (1 oz) salt

1 Quarter the apples, remove the cores and chop coarsely.

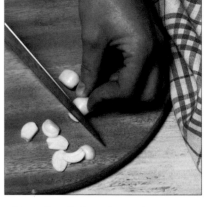

2 Peel and chop the garlic and place with the apple in a saucepan.

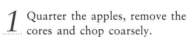

TIP
Unless you are using preserving jars with glass lids for pickles and chutneys, seal your jars with plastic or plastic-coated metal screw tops: do not use ordinary jam-pot covers as these allow the vinegar to evaporate, which will make the mixture shrink and become very dry within a few weeks.

3 Pour in enough vinegar to cover and boil gently until soft. Chop the dates and ginger and add them to the cooked apple and garlic, together with all the other ingredients. Simmer gently for 45 minutes. Spoon the mixture into warmed, sterilized jars and seal immediately. Store in a cool, dark place.

P.ICCALILLI

The piquancy of this bright yellow relish makes it an excellent partner for sausages, bacon and ham.

MAKES 1.5 KG (3½ LB)

675 g (1½ lb) cauliflower
450 g (1 lb) small onions
350 g (12 oz) French beans
5 ml (1 tsp) ground turmeric
5 ml (1 tsp) mustard powder
10 ml (2 tsp) cornflour (cornstarch)
600 ml (1 pint/2½ cups) vinegar

1 Cut the cauliflower into very small florets.

2 Peel the onions and trim the French beans.

TIP
Piccalilli will keep unopened for up to a year in a cool, dark place. Once opened, store in the fridge.

3 Put the turmeric, mustard and cornflour (cornstarch) in a small saucepan and pour over the vinegar. Stir well to blend, bring to the boil and simmer for 10 minutes.

4 Put the prepared vegetables in a large pan and pour over the vinegar mixture. Mix well and simmer for 45 minutes. Pour into warmed, sterilized jars and seal immediately.

APPLE & MINT JELLY

This jelly is a classic accompaniment to rich roasted lamb, and it is also delicious served with garden peas.

MAKES 1.5 KG (3½ LB)

900 g (2 lb) Bramley cooking apples
granulated sugar
45 ml (3 tbsp) chopped fresh mint

1 Chop the apples roughly and put them into a preserving pan. Add enough water to cover and simmer until the fruit is soft.

2 Strain through a jelly bag, allowing it to drip overnight. Do not squeeze the bag or the jelly will become cloudy.

3 Measure the amount of juice. To every 600 ml (1 pint/2½ cups), add 500 g (1¼ lb/2¼ cups) granulated sugar. Place the juice and sugar in a large pan and heat gently to dissolve the sugar. Bring to the boil.

4 After 10 minutes, test for setting by pouring about 5 ml (1 tsp) into a saucer and leaving to cool slightly. If a wrinkle forms on the surface when pushed with a fingertip, the jelly will set. Leave to cool.

5 Stir in the mint and pour the jelly into warmed, sterilized jars. Seal the jars immediately and store in a cool, dark place for up to a year.

YOGURT CHEESE IN OLIVE OIL

*Sheep's milk is widely used in cheese-making in the eastern Mediterranean,
particularly in Greece where sheep's yogurt is hung in cheesecloth to drain off the whey
before patting into balls of soft cheese. Here it is bottled in olive oil with chilli and herbs
to make an appetizing and beautiful gift.*

FILLS TWO 450 G (1 LB) JARS

750 g (1 ¾ lb) sheep's milk yogurt
2.5 ml (½ tsp) salt
10 ml (2 tsp) crushed dried chillies or
chilli powder
15 ml (1 tbsp) chopped fresh rosemary
15 ml (1 tbsp) chopped fresh thyme or
oregano
300 ml (½ pint/1¼ cups) olive oil,
preferably flavoured with garlic

1 Sterilize a 30 cm (12 in) square
of cheesecloth by steeping it in
boiling water. Squeeze out excess
water and lay over a large plate. Mix
the yogurt with the salt and tip into
the centre of the cheesecloth. Bring
up the sides and tie with string.

2 Hang the bag in a position where
you can place a bowl underneath
to catch the whey (from a kitchen
cupboard handle, for instance, with
the bowl on the worktop below).
Leave for 2–3 days until the yogurt
stops dripping.

3 Mix together the chilli and herbs.
Roll teaspoonfuls of the cheese
into balls between your hands. Put
into sterilized jars, sprinkling each
layer with the herb mixture.

4 Pour the oil over the cheeses
until completely covered.
Store the jars in the fridge for up
to 3 weeks. Serve with lightly
toasted bread.

TIP
If your kitchen is very warm, try
to find a cooler place to hang the
cheese while draining. If there is
space, suspend the bag from a shelf
in the fridge.

BOTTLED CHERRY TOMATOES

With fresh vegetables available all year round, we no longer need to rely on bottled vegetables, but with the addition of herbs and spices they can be turned from a staple to a luxury item. Cherry tomatoes bottled in their own juices with garlic and basil are sweetly delicious and a perfect accompaniment to thick slices of country ham.

FILLS TWO 1 LITRE (1¾ PINT/4 CUP) JARS

1 kg (2¼ lb) cherry tomatoes
5 ml (1 tsp) salt per 1 litre
(1¾ pint/4 cup) jar
5 ml (1 tsp) sugar per 1 litre
(1¾ pint/4 cup) jar
fresh basil
5 garlic cloves per 1 litre
(1¾ pint/4 cup) jar

1 Prick the skin of each tomato with a toothpick.

2 Pack the tomatoes into clean, dry jars, adding salt and sugar as you go.

3 Fill the jars to within 2 cm (¾ in) of the top and tuck the basil and garlic among the tomatoes. Rest the lids on the jars but do not seal. Stand them on a baking tray lined with a layer of card (cardboard) or newspaper in a low oven set at 120°C/250°F/Gas ½. After about 45 minutes, when the juice is simmering, remove the jars from the oven and seal. Store in a cool, dark place for up to 6 months.

GARLIC OIL

*This delicious oil can be used in salad dressings and to brush on
fish, meat and vegetables whenever you want a gentle garlic flavour. Hang a
garlic clove around the neck of the bottle to act as an identifying label.*

MAKES 750 ML (1¼ PINTS/3 CUPS)

*25 large, plump garlic cloves
900 ml (1½ pints/3¾ cups)
cold-pressed virgin olive oil*

TIP
Do not throw away the poached
garlic cloves when you remove
them from the oil: they are
ambrosial when spread on fresh
French bread or used as a relish
with meat, fish or vegetables.
Unless you are going to use them
immediately, pack them into a
glass jar, cover with fresh oil and
store in the fridge to use within
10 days.

1 Peel the garlic cloves. Pour the
olive oil into a saucepan.

2 Heat the oil to a gentle simmer,
then add the garlic cloves and
poach them for about 25 minutes,
until tender and transparent.

3 Leave the garlic cloves in the
saucepan until cool, then strain
them from the oil, reserving them for
another use. Pour the oil into a clean
bottle, seal with a screw top or cork
and use within 3 months.

RASPBERRY VINEGAR

*Raspberry vinegar gives a delicious depth to salad dressings and,
if used sparingly, will enhance the flavour of fruit such as strawberries and
nectarines that are not quite ripe.*

MAKES 750 ML (1¼ PINTS/3 CUPS)

600 ml (1 pint/2½ cups)
red wine vinegar
15 ml (1 tbsp) pickling spice
450 g (1 lb) raspberries, fresh or frozen
2 sprigs fresh lemon thyme

1 Pour the vinegar into a saucepan,
add the pickling spice and heat
gently for 5 minutes.

2 Pour the hot vinegar mixture
over the raspberries in a bowl
and then add the lemon thyme.

3 Cover and leave the mixture to
infuse for 2 days in a cool, dark
place, stirring occasionally. Strain
the liquid to remove the thyme and
raspberries, pour into a clean, dry
bottle and seal with a cork. Use
within 3 months.

ROSE PETAL VINEGAR

*This delicately scented vinegar can be used in a dressing for summer salads
and it is also effective as a cool compress to ease a nagging headache.*

MAKES 300 ML (½ PINT/1¼ CUPS)

*300 ml (½ pint/1 ¼ cups) white
wine vinegar
scented red roses*

1 Scald the vinegar by heating it
to just below boiling point, then
allow to cool. Pull the rose petals
from the flower heads. Snip away
the bitter white part at the base of
each petal. Prepare enough petals
to fill a cup and transfer to a glass
jar or bottle.

2 Add the cooled vinegar, cover
very tightly with a screw top
or cork, and leave on a sunny
windowsill for at least 3 weeks.

THYME & MUSTARD CRACKERS

Pack these aromatic digestive-type crackers into a basket with a selection of soft,
fresh cheeses to make a complete savoury gift.

MAKES ABOUT 40

175 g (6 oz/1½ cups) wholemeal
(whole wheat) flour
50 g (2 oz/½ cup) medium oatmeal
25 g (1 oz/2 tbsp) caster (superfine)
sugar
10 ml (2 tsp) baking powder
30 ml (2 tbsp) fresh thyme leaves
salt
freshly ground black pepper
50 g (2 oz/4 tbsp) butter
25 g (1 oz/2 tbsp) white vegetable fat
(shortening)
45 ml (3 tbsp) milk
10 ml (2 tsp) Dijon mustard
30 ml (2 tbsp) sesame seeds

1 Preheat the oven to 200°C/400°F/
Gas 6. Mix the flour, oatmeal,
sugar, baking powder, thyme and
seasoning in a bowl. Rub in the fats
to form fine crumbs. Mix the milk
and mustard, stir into the flour
mixture and continue mixing until
you have a soft but not sticky dough.

2 Knead lightly on a floured
surface, then roll out to a
thickness of 5 mm (¼ in). Stamp out
5 cm (2 in) rounds with a fluted
cutter and arrange on greased baking
sheets. Re-roll the trimmings and
continue stamping out biscuits until
all the dough is used. Prick the
biscuits with a fork and sprinkle
with sesame seeds. Cook for
10–12 minutes until lightly browned.
Cool on baking sheets, then pack in
an airtight container.

CRAB APPLE JELLY

Crab apple trees are very pretty with their abundant flowers and glowing fruits.
Though their role in the garden is mainly decorative, this beautiful jelly is a delicious way to
make use of the fruit. It is lovely served with game, and can be used to glaze an apple tart.

MAKES ABOUT 1 KG (2¼ LB) FROM EACH
600 ML (1 PINT/2½ CUPS) LIQUID

1 kg (2 ¼ lb) crab apples
3 cloves
preserving sugar

1 Wash the crab apples and cut them in half, but do not peel or core them.

2 Place with the cloves in a large saucepan and cover with water. Bring to the boil and simmer until soft.

3 Strain through a jelly bag, allowing it to drip overnight. Measure the amount of juice. To every 600 ml (1 pint/2½ cups) of juice, add 450 g (1 lb/2 cups) preserving sugar. Place the juice and sugar in a large pan and heat gently to dissolve the sugar. Increase the heat and boil rapidly until setting point is reached. Pour into warmed, sterilized jars and seal.

TIP

Test for setting by pouring about 5 ml (1 tsp) of jelly into a saucer and leaving to cool slightly. If a wrinkle forms on the surface when pushed with a fingertip, the jelly will set.

LEMON HERB MIX

This combination of lemon flavours makes a wonderful dry marinade
for chicken: rub it on to the skin about an hour before roasting or barbecuing.

MAKES ABOUT 50 G (2 OZ)

2 lemons
30 ml (2 tbsp) lemon thyme leaves
15 ml (1 tbsp) lemon verbena leaves
15 ml (1 tbsp) lemon grass, chopped

TIP
Traditionally, a mortar and pestle
are used to blend the herbs,
but using an electric coffee grinder
is an easy way to achieve very
good results.

1 Pare off the lemon rind in strips
and air-dry it with the herbs on
a rack for 1–2 days.

2 When thoroughly dry, powder
the lemon rind using a mortar
and pestle. Add the other flavourings
and crush and blend them together.

3 Pack the powdered herbs into
fabric bags and tie on a label
with instructions for their use.

CHOCOLATE TRUFFLES

*These are popular with almost everybody: simply use different combinations
of chocolate and flavourings to make an irresistible selection.*

MAKES 60

*115 g (4 oz) plain (semi-sweet)
chocolate
115 g (4 oz) milk chocolate
115 g (4 oz) white chocolate
175 ml (6 fl oz/¾ cup) double (heavy)
cream*

FLAVOURINGS
*30 ml (2 tbsp) dark rum
30 ml (2 tbsp) Tia Maria
30 ml (2 tbsp) apricot brandy*

COATINGS
*50 g (2 oz) coarsely grated plain
(semi-sweet) chocolate
50 g (2 oz) coarsely grated milk
chocolate
50 g (2 oz) coarsely grated white
chocolate*

1 Melt each type of chocolate in a separate bowl. Heat the cream gently in a small saucepan until hot but not boiling. Allow to cool. Stir one-third of the cream into each of the bowls and blend evenly. Add the rum to the plain (semi-sweet) chocolate and whisk until the mixture becomes lighter in colour. Whisk the Tia Maria into the milk chocolate and, lastly, whisk the apricot brandy into the white chocolate.

2 Allow the three mixtures to thicken, giving them an occasional stir, until they are thick enough to divide into equal spoonfuls. Line three baking sheets with baking parchment. Place about 16 teaspoonfuls of each chocolate mixture, well spaced apart, on the baking sheets and chill until the mixture is firm enough to roll into small balls with your hands.

3 Place each of the grated chocolates in separate dishes. Shape the dark chocolate truffles into neat balls and roll in grated plain (semi-sweet) chocolate to coat evenly. Repeat with the milk chocolate truffles and grated milk chocolate, and the white chocolate truffles and grated white chocolate. Chill the truffles until firm, then arrange in boxes, bags or tins and tie with festive ribbon.

DOUBLE CHOCOLATE-DIPPED FRUIT

*Just about any kind of fruit can be dipped in chocolate as long as the fruit is dry:
even one drop of moisture can cause the melted chocolate to seize and harden. Choose fresh fruits
if you can make these chocolates on the day you are giving them, but dried fruits or nuts
are also delicious if you are making them in advance.*

MAKES 24 PIECES

*fruits – about 24 pieces
(strawberries, cherries, orange
segments, large seedless grapes,
Cape gooseberries, kumquats, stoned
prunes, dried apricots, dried
pears or nuts)
115 g (4 oz) fine quality white
chocolate, chopped
115 g (4 oz) fine quality bitter
(bittersweet) or plain (semi-sweet)
chocolate, chopped*

1 Clean and prepare the fruits: wipe strawberries with a soft cloth or brush gently with a pastry brush. Wash firm-skinned fruits such as cherries and grapes; dry well and set on paper towels to absorb any remaining moisture. Remove all traces of pith from orange segments. Melt the white chocolate in a bowl over hot water or in a double boiler, then cool to tepid (about 30°C/88°F), stirring frequently.

2 Line a baking sheet with baking parchment. Holding each piece of fruit by the stem or end and at an angle, dip about two-thirds into the chocolate. Allow the excess to drip off and place on the baking sheet. (If the chocolate becomes too thick, set it over hot water again to soften slightly.) Refrigerate the fruits until the chocolate sets, about 20 minutes.

3 Melt the dark chocolate in the cleaned double boiler over a low heat, stirring frequently until smooth. Remove from the heat and cool to just below body temperature, approximately 30°C/88°F.

4 Take each white chocolate-coated fruit and, holding at the opposite angle, dip the bottom third of each piece into the dark chocolate, creating a chevron effect. Set on a baking sheet and refrigerate for 15 minutes or until set.

PEPPERMINT CHOCOLATE STICKS

Elegant, slim dark chocolate sticks, studded with pieces of crisp peppermint brittle,
make a perfect accompaniment to after-dinner coffee.

MAKES ABOUT 80

115 g (4 oz/½ cup) granulated sugar
150 ml (¼ pint/⅔ cup) water
2.5 ml (½ tsp) peppermint
essence (extract)
200 g (7 oz) plain (semi-sweet)
chocolate, broken into squares
60 ml (4 tbsp) toasted desiccated
(shredded) coconut

TIP
The set chocolate mixture could be
cut into squares if you prefer.
They make good decorations for
cakes and desserts.

1 Lightly oil a large baking sheet.
Place the sugar and water in a
small, heavy-based saucepan and heat
gently, stirring occasionally, until the
sugar has dissolved completely. Bring
to the boil and boil rapidly without
stirring until the syrup registers
138°C/280°F on a sugar thermometer.

2 Remove the pan from the heat
and add the peppermint essence
(extract), then pour on to the oiled
baking sheet and leave until set and
completely cold. Break up the
peppermint mixture into a small
bowl and use the end of a rolling pin
to crush it into small pieces.

3 Melt the chocolate in a bowl
over hot water. Remove from the
heat and stir in the mint pieces and
desiccated coconut. Lay a 30 x 25 cm
(12 x 10 in) sheet of baking
parchment on a flat surface. Spread
the chocolate mixture over the paper,
leaving a narrow border all around,
to make a rectangle measuring about
25 x 20 cm (10 x 8 in). Leave to set.
When firm, use a sharp knife to cut
into thin sticks, each about 6 cm
(2 ¼ in) long.

THREE-FRUIT MARMALADE

Home-made marmalade may be time-consuming to make, but the results are incomparably better than store-bought varieties. This tangy version can be made at any time of the year.

MAKES 4 KG (9 LB)

350 g (12 oz) oranges
350 g (12 oz) lemons
675 g (1½ lb) grapefruit
2.5 litres (4½ pints/10¼ cups) water
2.75 kg (6 lb/12 cups) granulated sugar

1. Scrub all the fruit thoroughly with a vegetable brush, and rinse.

2. Put the fruit in a preserving pan. Add the water and simmer, uncovered, for about 2 hours.

3. When the fruit is very tender and the liquid has reduced to about half its original volume, remove the fruit and quarter it. Scrape out the pulp, extracting any pips, and return it to the pan with the cooking liquid.

4. Cut the rinds into slivers, and add to the pan. Add the sugar and heat gently until dissolved, then bring to the boil and cook until setting point is reached. Leave to stand for 1 hour. Pour into sterilized jars and seal immediately. Store in a cool, dark place.

TIP
Test for setting by pouring about 5 ml (1 tsp) into a saucer and leaving to cool slightly. If a wrinkle forms on the surface when pushed with a fingertip, the marmalade will set.

STRAWBERRY JAM

*This classic recipe is always popular. Make sure the jam is allowed to cool
before pouring it into jars so that the fruit does not float to the top.*

MAKES 2.25 KG (5 LB)

*1.5 kg (3½ lb) strawberries
1.5 kg (3½ lb/6 cups) granulated sugar
juice of ½ lemon*

1 Hull the strawberries and mash
a few of them. Warm the sugar
in a bowl in a low oven (120°C/
250°F/Gas ½).

2 Put the mashed and whole
strawberries in a preserving pan
with the lemon juice and bring to a
gentle simmer.

TIP
Test for setting by pouring about
5 ml (1 tsp) into a saucer and
leaving to cool slightly. If a
wrinkle forms on the surface when
pushed with a fingertip, the jam
will set.

3 Add the warmed sugar and let it
dissolve slowly over a gentle
heat. Then let the jam boil rapidly
until setting point is reached. Remove
from the heat.

4 Leave to cool, then stir until the
strawberries are well distributed
through the jam. Pour into warmed,
sterilized jars and seal immediately.

LEMON & LIME CURD

*Limes add extra zest to this old-fashioned spread, which
is wonderfully enlivening on toast or muffins. The curd will keep unopened for up to
a month. Once opened, keep it in the fridge and consume within a week.*

MAKES 900 G (2 LB)
....
115 g *(4 oz/½ cup) unsalted
(sweet) butter*
*3 eggs
grated rind and juice of 2 lemons
grated rind and juice of 2 limes*
225 g *(8 oz/1⅛ cups) caster
(superfine) sugar*

1 Set a bowl over a large pan of
simmering water. Add the butter.

2 Lightly beat the eggs and add
them to the butter.

3 Add the lemon and lime rinds
and juices, then add the sugar.

4 Stir the mixture constantly until
it thickens. Pour into sterilized
jars and seal immediately. Store in a
cool, dark place.

RHUBARB & GINGER PRESERVE

Ginger is a traditional flavouring for rhubarb jam, but in this recipe
the flavour is boosted further by the addition of ginger mint, which is easily grown in the garden.
The soft pink of the preserve is prettily set off by the fresh green flecks of the herb.

MAKES 2.75 KG (6 LB)

2 kg (4 lb) rhubarb
250 ml (8 fl oz/1 cup) water
juice of 1 lemon
5 cm (2 in) piece fresh root ginger
1.5 kg (3½ lb/6 cups) sugar
115 g (4 oz/⅔ cup) preserved stem
ginger, chopped
30–45 ml (2–3 tbsp) very finely
chopped ginger mint leaves

TIP
Test for setting by pouring about
5 ml (1 tsp) into a saucer and
leaving to cool slightly. If a
wrinkle forms on the surface when
pushed with a fingertip, the jam
will set.

1 Wash and trim the rhubarb,
cutting it into small pieces about
2.5 cm (1 in) long. Place the rhubarb,
water and lemon juice in a preserving
pan and bring to the boil. Peel and
bruise the piece of fresh root ginger
and add it to the pan. Simmer,
stirring frequently, until the rhubarb
is soft. Remove the ginger.

2 Add the sugar and stir until it
has dissolved. Bring the mixture
to the boil and boil rapidly for
10–15 minutes, or until setting point
is reached. With a metal slotted
spoon, remove any scum from the
surface of the jam. Add the stem
ginger and ginger mint leaves. Pour
into warmed, sterilized jars and seal.

CANDIED PEEL RIBBONS

Home-made candied peel is so delicious that it can be eaten on its own,
as a sweetmeat. Make it in the latter part of winter when the new season's citrus fruit arrives:
it will keep all year round. The same process may be used to candy orange slices and
larger pieces of citrus peel.

MAKES ABOUT 675 G (1½ LB)

5 large oranges or 10 lemons or limes,
unwaxed
675 g (1½ lb/3 cups) granulated sugar,
plus extra for sprinkling

1 Halve the fruit, squeeze out the juice and reserve for another use. Discard the flesh of the fruit, but not the pith.

2 Cut the peel into strips about 1 cm (½ in) wide and place in a pan. Cover with boiling water and simmer for 5 minutes. Drain, then repeat four times, using fresh water each time to remove the peel's bitterness.

TIP

To preserve the individual flavour of each fruit – lemons, limes and oranges – they should all be candied separately. Any syrup that is left over can be used in fruit salads or drizzled over a freshly baked sponge cake.

3 Put the sugar in a heavy-based saucepan, pour 250 ml (8 fl oz/ 1 cup) water over it and heat gently, stirring, to dissolve. Add the peel and cook slowly, partially covered, for 30–40 minutes or until soft. Leave to cool completely, then sprinkle with sugar.

FONDANT HEARTS

Steal a heart on Valentine's Day with these luscious love tokens.
Instead of the drizzled chocolate, you could pipe some decorations –
your entwined initials, perhaps?

MAKES ABOUT 50

60 ml (4 tbsp) liquid glucose
50 g (2 oz) plain (semi-sweet)
chocolate, broken into squares
50 g (2 oz) white chocolate, broken
into squares
1 egg white, lightly beaten
450 g (1 lb/4 cups) icing
(confectioners') sugar, sifted
melted dark and white chocolate,
to decorate

1 Divide the glucose between two bowls placed over hot water and heat gently, then add the dark chocolate to one bowl and the white chocolate to the other. Leave until the chocolate has melted completely. Remove both bowls from the heat and cool slightly. Reserve a small amount of the egg white, then divide the rest between the two bowls. Add half of the icing (confectioners') sugar to each bowl, mixing to combine well.

2 Knead each mixture separately with your hands until it is smooth and pliable. On a surface lightly dusted with icing (confectioners') sugar, roll out both mixtures separately to a thickness of about 3 mm (⅛ in).

TIP
Do not throw away the fondant trimmings – knead them together to create a marbled effect, roll the fondant out again and cut out more hearts or other shapes to use as cake decorations.

3 Brush the surface of the dark chocolate fondant with the reserved egg white and place the white chocolate fondant on top. Roll the surface lightly with a rolling pin to press the pieces together.

4 Using a heart-shaped cutter, stamp out about 50 hearts from the fondant. Drizzle melted chocolate over each heart to decorate and leave in a cool place until firm.

EASTER LOAF

If you are visiting friends at Easter, take this jewelled fruit loaf for your hosts
as an alternative to a chocolate egg. Presented in a napkin-lined basket, it will make an original and
beautiful gift. It is delicious served sliced with butter and jam, and is also very good toasted
on the following day.

SERVES 8

200 ml (7 fl oz/⅞ cup) milk
2 eggs
450 g (1 lb/4 cups) plain
(all-purpose) flour
2.5 ml (½ tsp) salt
10 ml (2 tsp) ground mixed spice
75 g (3 oz/6 tbsp) butter
75 g (3 oz/6 tbsp) caster
(superfine) sugar
20 g (¾ oz) dried yeast
175 g (6 oz/1¼ cups) currants
25 g (1 oz/¼ cup) candied mixed peel,
chopped
a little sweetened milk, to glaze
25 g (1 oz/1½ tbsp) glacé (candied)
cherries, chopped
15 g (½ oz/1 tbsp) candied angelica,
chopped

1 Heat the milk until it is lukewarm, add two-thirds of it to the eggs and mix well. Sift the flour, salt and mixed spice together. Rub in the butter, then add the sugar and dried yeast. Make a well in the centre and add the milk mixture, adding more milk as necessary to make a sticky dough.

3 Turn the dough out on to a floured surface and knead again for 2–3 minutes. Divide the dough into three equal pieces. Roll each piece into a sausage shape roughly 20 cm (8 in) long. Plait the three pieces together, turning under and pinching each end. Place on a floured baking sheet and leave to rise for 15 minutes.

2 Knead on a well-floured surface and then knead in the currants and mixed peel, reserving 15 ml (1 tbsp) of mixed peel for the topping. Put the dough in a lightly greased bowl and cover it with a damp cloth. Leave the dough until it has doubled in size. Preheat the oven to 220°C/425°F/Gas 7.

4 Brush the top of the plait with a little sweetened milk and scatter with roughly chopped glacé (candied) cherries, small strips of angelica and the reserved mixed peel. Bake in the preheated oven for 45 minutes or until the loaf sounds hollow when tapped on the bottom. Leave to cool on a wire rack before packing.

TRUFFLE-FILLED EASTER EGG

Moulding your own chocolate Easter egg is very rewarding and makes a special gift.
Pack the finished egg in a box or wrap it lavishly in gold foil or sparkling cellophane
(plastic wrap) tied with ribbons.

MAKES 1 LARGE HOLLOW EASTER EGG

350 g (12 oz) plain (semi-sweet),
milk or white chocolate, melted
truffles to fill (optional)
(see Chocolate Truffles recipe)
2 x 15 cm (6 in) plastic Easter
egg moulds

1 Line a small baking sheet with baking parchment. Using a small ladle or spoon, pour in enough melted chocolate to coat the moulds. Tilt the moulds slowly to coat the sides. Set the moulds, open side down, on the prepared baking sheet. Refrigerate for 1–2 minutes until just set. Apply a second coat of chocolate and refrigerate for 1–3 minutes until set. (Reheat the chocolate gently if it hardens.) Repeat a third time and refrigerate for at least 1 hour or until completely set.

2 To unmould the egg, trim any drops of chocolate from the edge of the mould. Gently insert the point of a knife between the chocolate and the mould to break the air lock. Holding the mould open side down, squeeze firmly to release the half egg. Repeat with the other half and refrigerate, loosely covered. (Do not touch the surface of the chocolate with your fingers as they will leave prints.) Reserve any melted chocolate to reheat to stick the two halves together.

3 To assemble the egg, hold one half with a piece of folded paper towel or foil and fill with small truffles. Spread a small amount of the remaining melted chocolate on to the rim of the half egg and, holding the other half with a piece of paper towel or foil, press it on, making sure the rims match up.

4 Hold for several seconds, then prop the egg up with the folded paper towel or foil and refrigerate to set. Wrap the egg in foil or cellophane (plastic wrap) and decorate with ribbons or Easter decorations.

PUMPKIN PIE

*The food and decorations for Hallowe'en are supposed to echo the occasion,
with the decorations being scary and the food bringing comfort. Pumpkins are the main
attraction as they are transformed into glowing lanterns and their flesh is made into
soups, pies and fritters.*

SERVES 8

450 g (1 lb) pumpkin
175 g (6 oz/¾ cup) brown sugar
175 ml (6 fl oz/¾ cup) milk
4 eggs
*250 ml (8 fl oz/1 cup) double (heavy)
cream*
50 ml (2 fl oz/¼ cup) brandy
10 ml (2 tsp) ground cinnamon
*2.5 ml (½ tsp) ground ginger or
grated nutmeg*
2.5 ml (½ tsp) salt
*25 cm (10 in) flan tin lined with
shortcrust pastry, chilled*

1 Remove the pumpkin flesh
from the shell and chop it into
small cubes.

2 Steam the cubed pumpkin for
about 10–15 minutes until soft,
and leave to drain, preferably
overnight.

3 Preheat the oven to 180°C/350°F/
Gas 4. Place the pumpkin in a
food processor with all the remaining
filling ingredients and blend to a
smooth texture. Pour into the
prepared pastry case and bake for
1¼ hours.

TIP
Use a pastry cutter to cut star
patterns in the hollowed-out shell
of your pumpkin to make a table
decoration.

HARVEST LOAF

The harvest loaf is the traditional centrepiece of the church at harvest festival,
displayed at the altar among the fruit and vegetables and other offerings. Although many different
designs are used, the most enduringly popular is the wheatsheaf, symbolic of the harvest and
the vital importance of bread as "the staff of life".

MAKES TWO 750 G (1¾ LB) LOAVES

1.5 kg (3½ lb/12 cups) strong
white flour
30 ml (2 tbsp) salt
15 g (½ oz/1 tbsp) dried yeast
sugar, to activate yeast
beaten egg, to glaze

1 Sift the flour and salt together into a bowl and make a well. Mix the yeast with 105 ml (7 tbsp) warm water and a little sugar and leave to activate for 15 minutes. Add the yeast mixture and 750 ml (1¼ pints/3 cups) water to the flour and mix thoroughly using your hands. Turn out on to a floured surface and knead until the dough becomes elastic. Place the dough in a lightly oiled bowl, cover and leave to prove for 1–2 hours, until it has doubled in size.

TIP
The high salt content in the dough makes it easier to work but not very palatable. If you want to eat the finished loaf, reduce the amount of salt to just a pinch.

2 Preheat the oven to 220°C/ 425°F/Gas 7. Take about 225 g (8 oz) of the dough and roll it into a 30 cm (12 in) long cylinder. Place it on a large oiled and floured baking sheet and flatten it slightly with your hand. This will form the base for the long stalks of the wheatsheaf.

3 Take about 350 g (12 oz) of the remaining dough, roll and shape it into a crescent. Place this at the top of the cylinder and flatten. Divide the remaining dough in half. Divide one half in two again. Use one half to make the stalks of the wheat by rolling into narrow ropes and placing on the "stalk" of the sheaf. Use the other half to make a plait to decorate the finished loaf where the stalks meet the ears of wheat.

4 Use the remaining dough to make the ears of wheat. Roll it into small sausage shapes and snip each one a few times with scissors to give the effect of the separate ears. Place these on the crescent shape, fanning out from the base until the wheatsheaf is complete. Position the plait between the stalks and the ears of wheat. Brush the wheatsheaf with the beaten egg. Bake for 20 minutes, then reduce the heat to 160°C/325°F/Gas 3 and bake for a further 20 minutes.

CHRISTMAS KISSES

These rich little biscuits look attractive mixed together on a plate, thickly dusted
with sugar. Serve them with coffee, or as an accompaniment to ice cream.

MAKES 14

75 g (3 oz) plain (semi-sweet)
chocolate, broken into pieces
75 g (3 oz) white chocolate, broken
into pieces
115 g (4 oz/½ cup) butter
115 g (4 oz/8 tbsp) caster (superfine)
sugar
2 eggs
225 g (8 oz/2 cups) plain flour
icing (confectioners') sugar,
to decorate

1 Put each chocolate into a
separate small bowl and melt it
over a pan of barely simmering
water. Set aside to cool.

2 Beat together the butter and
caster (superfine) sugar until pale
and fluffy. Beat in the eggs, one at a
time. Sift in the flour and mix well.

3 Divide the mixture between the
two bowls of chocolate. Mix in
each chocolate thoroughly. Knead the
doughs until smooth, wrap them in
clear film (plastic wrap) and chill
them for 1 hour. Preheat the oven to
190°C/375°F/Gas 5.

4 Take up slightly rounded
teaspoonfuls of each dough
and roll into balls in the palms of
your hands. Arrange them on
greased baking trays and bake for
10–12 minutes. Dust with sifted icing
(confectioners') sugar and transfer to
a wire rack to cool.

SPICED CHRISTMAS CAKE

This light cake mixture is flavoured with spices and fruit.
Dust it delicately with icing (confectioners') sugar and decorate it with a sprig
of holly before packing it into a box to make a delightful
Christmas surprise.

MAKES 1 CAKE

225 g (8 oz/1 cup) butter, plus extra
for greasing
15 g (½ oz/1 tbsp) fresh white breadcrumbs
225 g (8 oz/1 cup) caster (superfine)
sugar
50 ml (2 fl oz/¼ cup) water
3 eggs, separated
225 g (8 oz/2 cups) self-raising flour
7.5 ml (1½ tsp) ground
mixed spice
25 g (1 oz/2 tbsp) candied angelica,
chopped
25 g (1 oz/2 tbsp) candied mixed peel
50 g (2 oz/¼ cup) glacé (candied)
cherries, chopped
50 g (2 oz/½ cup) walnuts, chopped
icing (confectioners') sugar, to dust

1 Preheat the oven to 180°C/350°F/
Gas 4. Brush a 20 cm (8 in),
1.5 litre (2½ pint) fluted ring mould
with melted butter and coat with
fresh white breadcrumbs. Tip the
mould to cover the sides completely,
then shake out any excess crumbs.

2 Place the butter, sugar and water
in a saucepan and heat gently,
stirring occasionally, until melted.
Boil for 3 minutes until syrupy, then
allow to cool. Whisk the egg whites
until stiff. Sift the flour and spice
into a bowl, add the angelica, mixed
peel, cherries and walnuts and stir
well to mix. Add the egg yolks.

3 Pour the cooled butter and sugar
mixture into the bowl and beat
together with a wooden spoon to
form a soft batter. Gradually fold in
the egg whites, using a plastic
spatula, until the mixture is evenly
blended. Pour into the prepared
mould and bake for 50–60 minutes
or until the cake springs back when
pressed in the centre. Turn out and
cool on a wire rack.

INDIVIDUAL DUNDEE CAKES

Dundee cakes are traditionally topped with almonds,
but also look tempting covered with glacé (candied) fruits. One of these small cakes
would make a charming gift for someone living alone, or could be included in
a Christmas hamper (package).

MAKES 3 CAKES

225 g (8 oz/1 cup) raisins
225 g (8 oz/1 cup) currants
225 g (8 oz/1 cup) sultanas
50 g (2 oz/¼ cup) glacé (candied)
cherries, sliced
115 g (4 oz/¾ cup) candied mixed peel
grated rind of 1 orange
300 g (11 oz/2¾ cups) plain
(all-purpose) flour
2.5 ml (½ tsp) baking powder
5 ml (1 tsp) ground mixed spice
225 g (8 oz/1 cup) unsalted (sweet)
butter, softened
225 g (8 oz/1 cup) caster
(superfine) sugar
5 eggs

TOPPING

50 g (2 oz/½ cup) whole blanched
almonds
50 g (2 oz/¼ cup) glacé (candied)
cherries, halved
50 g (2 oz/½ cup) glacé (candied)
fruits, sliced
45 ml (3 tbsp) apricot jam

TIP

To make a glaze for the tops of the
cakes, add 30 ml (2 tbsp) water to
the apricot jam in a small pan.
Heat gently, stirring, to melt the
jam, and sieve.

1 Preheat the oven to 150°C/
300°F/Gas 2. Grease and line
three 15 cm (6 in) round cake tins
and tie a strip of brown parcel wrap
(packaging paper) around each. Mix
all the fruit and the orange rind in a
large mixing bowl. In another bowl,
sift the flour, baking powder and
mixed spice. Add the butter, sugar
and eggs. Mix together with
a wooden spoon and beat for
2–3 minutes until smooth and glossy.

2 Add the mixed fruit to the cake
mixture and fold in using a
spatula until well blended. Divide the
cake mixture between the three tins
and level the tops. Arrange the
almonds in circles over the top of one
cake, the glacé (candied) cherries over
the second cake and the mixed glacé
(candied) fruits over the last one.
Bake in the oven for 2–2½ hours or
until a skewer inserted into the centre
of the cakes comes out clean.

3 Leave the cakes in their tins
until completely cold. Turn out,
remove the lining paper and brush
the tops with apricot glaze. Leave to
set, then wrap in cellophane or clear
film (plastic wrap) and pack in
pretty boxes or tins.

HEARTS & HANDS COOKIES

A classic token of love for any time of the year, these delicious gingerbread cookies can also be turned into charming folk-art decorations, using scraps of fabric, ribbons and buttons. They make wonderful Christmas tree decorations.

INGREDIENTS

350 g (12 oz/3 cups) plain flour
5 ml (1 tsp) ground cinnamon
5 ml (1 tsp) ground ginger
2.5 ml (½ tsp) ground allspice
50 g (2 oz/¼ cup) soft brown sugar
45 ml (3 tbsp) golden syrup (corn syrup)
45 ml (3 tbsp) black treacle (molasses)
50 g (2 oz/4 tbsp) butter, softened
2.5 ml (½ tsp) bicarbonate of soda (baking soda)
15 ml (1 tbsp) warm water
1 egg, beaten
royal icing

MATERIALS

garden twine
cotton gingham fabric
glue gun or all-purpose glue
buttons
ribbons
picture-hanging hook
card (cardboard)

TIP

Large cookies need careful handling – if they are to be used as decorations, glue a sheet of card (cardboard) on the back to reinforce them. Glue a picture hook on the back if you wish to hang a cookie on the wall.

1 Sift the flour and spices into a bowl. Beat the sugar, treacle (molasses), syrup and butter together. Mix the bicarbonate of soda (baking soda) and water, and add to the sugar mixture. Add the beaten egg and mix well. Add the flour mixture, a little at a time, and mix until you have a firm dough. Knead gently and allow to rest for 30 minutes. Roll out thinly on a floured board.

2 Preheat the oven to 180°C/350°F/ Gas 4. Cut out the shapes and bake on a baking sheet lined with baking parchment for 10–15 minutes. Make a hole for hanging the cookies or a pattern of holes, if you wish, while they are warm, then allow to cool completely. For edible cookies, decorate with white royal icing, using a piping bag or syringe and a fine writing nozzle.

3 If the cookies are not going to be eaten, put them back in a low oven for a couple of hours to dry out so they will keep longer. String some together with garden twine. Make bows for tying from fabric for some; cut out heart motifs and glue them on others. If you wish to tone down the colour of the gingham, soak it in tea. Decorate the ties with buttons and ribbons.

HOGMANAY SHORTBREAD

This deliciously light Hogmanay, or New Year's Eve, shortbread is based on a traditional Scottish recipe.

MAKES 2 LARGE OR
8 INDIVIDUAL SHORTBREADS

175 g (6 oz/1½ cups) plain
(all-purpose) flour
50 g (2 oz/¼ cup) cornflour
(cornstarch)
50 g (2 oz/¼ cup) caster
(superfine) sugar
115 g (4 oz/½ cup) unsalted (sweet)
butter
sugar, to decorate

1 Preheat the oven to 160°C/325°F/ Gas 3. Lightly flour a mould and line a baking sheet with baking parchment. Sift the flour, cornflour (cornstarch) and sugar into a mixing bowl. Cut the butter into pieces and rub into the flour mixture until you can knead it into a soft dough.

2 Place some dough in the floured shortbread mould and press to fit neatly. Invert the mould on to the baking sheet and tap firmly to release the dough shape. Repeat with the rest of the dough. Bake in the oven for 35–40 minutes or until the shortbread is pale golden in colour.

TIP
Handle the dough as little as possible to avoid making the shortbread tough. If you do not have a wooden mould, press the dough into a round flan tin or ring and crimp the edges.

3 Sprinkle the top of the short- bread with a little sugar and cool on the baking sheet. Wrap in cellophane (plastic wrap) or place in a box tied with ribbon.

INDEX

Acknowledgements
The publishers would like to thank the
following people for designing and
making the projects in this book:
Penny Boylan, Jacqueline Clark, Stephanie
Donaldson, Tessa Evelegh, Joanna
Farrow, Christine France, Gilly Love,
Sue Maggs, Janice Murfitt, Katherine
Richmond, Liz Trigg, Elizabeth Wolf-
Cohen, Sally Walton, Stewart Walton,
Juliet Bawden.
Photographers:
Karl Adamson, Edward Allwright,
Steve Baxter, John Freeman, Michelle
Garrett, Debbie Patterson, Steve Tanner,
Polly Wreford

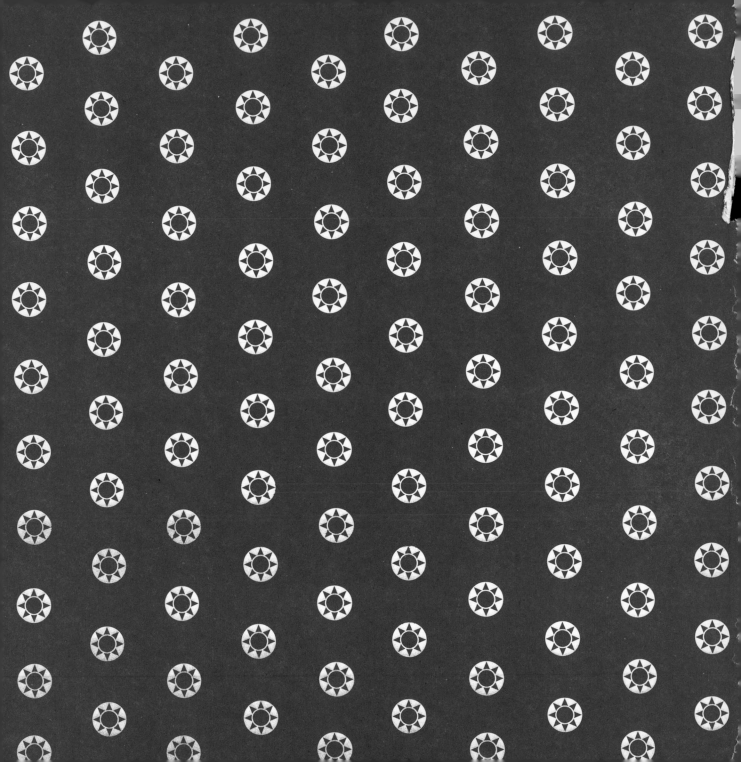